Top Squad

Essentials of an Excellent Team

Precious Eda

ISBN 978-93-5610-235-4
© Precious Eda 2022
Published in India 2022 by Pencil

A brand of
One Point Six Technologies Pvt. Ltd.
123, Building J2, Shram Seva Premises,
Wadala Truck Terminal, Wadala (E)
Mumbai 400037, Maharashtra, INDIA
E connect@thepencilapp.com
W www.thepencilapp.com

DISCLAIMER: *The opinions expressed in this book are those of the authors and do not purport to reflect the views of the Publisher.*

Author biography

*** Precious Eda is a leader with a passion for seeing people become better than they already are. He believes in and pursues his life-purpose which is to add value to everyone he meets.

With over 15 years spent in leading young people at various levels, he lives with a commitment towards growing more leaders through teaching leadership and personal development.

A Speaker, Teacher, Mentor to many and a trained Attorney.

*** His series of mini-books that treat singular issues in the very vast subject of leadership in each of it's series.

It is designed to make key issues and principles in leadership easy to understand and apply to everyday situations.

*** Top Squad is part of a series of mini-books that treat single points in the very vast topic of leadership in each of it's publications.

*** Other books in the series include :

Vision, The Core, How to Beat Your Leader

*** Precious Eda is blessed to share his life with Amarachi Loveth his amazing wife.

CONTENTS

Preface

I got involved with leadership at group levels quite early. Say at about the age of14 I held a position on the executive council of the teenagers fellowship in my local Church – the D/Line Branch of The Church of God Mission International in Port Harcourt. Honestly and obviously, I had no knowledge whatsoever of what it meant to lead people or be part of group of leaders. At that time it was just something of much fun to be put up for an election and have most of the girls vote to make me win by a majority. Elections were organised and conducted by the Assistant Pastor at that time. I remember him quite well – Rev. Iselema David-West. A very Spirit-filled, intelligent and eloquent excellent preacher he was and still is. He was in charge of getting a leadership team together for the teenagers in church and overseeing their growth and relevance to the church community.

At that time, our role as teenagers wasn't so huge; we simply had to meet and plan an event each year that would have every teenager in church take part in one activity or another. We just had to draw up a programme of activities that would occupy us for at least three days in a week for the chosen week in the year. Drawing up the programme was easy cos we had precedents – we had seen how it had been done by our predecessors and in other branches of our church, so we always had a good idea of how the teenagers' week would turn out.

So while the elections were going on, we had lofty concepts flying through our minds on how our time as leaders would be different and special, and how we would no doubt do better than others, and how we couldn't just wait to hit the ground running to bring to birth all the plans we had in mind. But you know, we haven't reached the interesting part, I'm sure you can guess that. All the fires of excitement would soon quench in the face of reality. In a few months' time I realised that we were only about four persons who ran the group and this was out of about 12 Executive Council members. All the plans and ideas we had birthed as a council were being executed by just a few of us.

Then we began to see failures creep in. We couldn't organise the yearly event for that first year and the year passed. Admittedly, we were all students in Secondary School and we had to go back to school. A good number of us attended boarding schools so it meant we always had limited time to plan and execute plans. But we always failed to take advantage of the holidays and we just couldn't make the difference we thought we could make.

This work was not intended for telling the full story of my young leadership experience as a teenager, but I had to summarise that experience in order to lay the proper foundation for what we will deal with in this mini-book. The relevance of that summary to this work is that when I got into the University and got thrust into leadership again, I had to draw from those teenage years the lessons that taught me how to succeed as a leader on a higher level. At the University, there were new lessons to be learnt and new experiences to be gotten, but the art of team-work had been imprinted in my heart and the challenge of the moment was not in trying to work with a team but how to effectively reach success with my team.

The challenges with succeeding with a team are immense; getting a vision that would be appealing to everyone, getting everyone to run with the vision, effectively having everyone take responsibility for their role in the team, changing team members when it is obviously necessary, not pleasing everyone but making sure everyone is happy and having team members step up for each other. There is always a difference between having a team that is ready to work and having a team that is willing to succeed.

In this work, I've tried to make things simple by helping us realise or rather reemphasise the importance of not being a lone ranger in pursuing your purpose and how to enlist the services of an excellent team or be a resourceful member of an excellent group. In simple and easy to apply principles, we consider how to become more effective as a group than alone.

I believe no person alive can reach the zenith of their full potentials by being a lone ranger. That's why I've written this book to share the principles that have helped great achievers succeed. I hope it stays as an asset of great value to you and helps you reach the topmost heights of your potentials.

Acknowledgements

DEDICATION

To Chelsea FC

The football club with the greatest team in the world

And

To the greatest teammate ever,

My Wife and Best Friend, Loveth

NO LONE RANGING: REACHING SUCCESS THROUGH HARNESSING THE POWER OF TEAMWORK

Introduction

Well, I've talked on several occasions on this issue of excellence and as it shows without any doubts that there's really no hard and fast rule to reaching excellent heights in any endeavour. Anyone with the right mind-set and genuine desire for perfection and superior quality could attain it. Of course, there are similarities in actions with most successful people, but these people would tell general "on the surface" perceptions. If deep details are sought, it would reveal some differences. However, for any leader who is people oriented and aims at reaching excellent heights with his people rather than with himself alone, it is important to consider some essential ideas that could help in realizing your vision.

So, I have thought out some well observed ideas which from experience I think have helped shaped my leadership over the years. I've learnt from both participating and observing. So, I think it's important to share these ideas and hopefully they would help us get better with our people. And yes! People! Leadership without people is nothing. Dr Myles Munroe once said "a leader who has no one following him is only taking a walk". That's truly how it feels being a lone ranger. You're merely taking a walk.

For everyone who dares to be different from the rest of the world, you must never underestimate the power of people. And the moment you begin to enlist the help of people in reaching you goals, you begin to pave the way for the necessity of teamwork and the benefits attached to it.

I follow sports a lot and I must say, since 1996, there's never been an Olympic Games I failed to follow. Apart from soccer, athletics is a favourite sport for me. I picked interest in long distance running while watching the Sydney Olympic Games. I recall watching the ten thousand meters race and seeing how the East African runners dominated proceedings. The excitement was something else. I watched how one little man called Haile Gabrille Selassie intelligently ran that race and won gold.

The interesting lesson from that race was that though the race was an individual competition, of course only three winners would emerge, the East Africans really ran as a team. You could see the cooperation and organisation they expressed on the track. This was and continues to be one major distinguishing factor between the African runners and their European counterparts. During the race which lasted almost an hour or more, you could see the East Africans take turns at leading the race, you could visibly see them talk to themselves while running and whisper instructions to each other. Of course, when it came to the moment that would define the three winners, you would think they had turned enemies in a few minutes. But essentially, their aim was to ensure they were in front and led the race for as long as they could so that when it got to the final laps of the race, only they would be in the perfect position to sweep the medals. And so it went, the Africans swept and have always swept the medals. This was an individual competition, but with the tool of teamwork in one hand, the athletes had fashioned out a method of ensuring that only Africans finished tops.

So, the truth is, no matter how good you think you are or how strong, smart or skilful you may think you are, without people you are nothing, and without teamwork you are a lone ranger and lone rangers always die alone. I hope that we can learn the good lesson that no matter what kind of dream you choose to pursue as a leader, you can only reach it with teamwork.

I. PURPOSE

In fact, it is almost like an A B C format. You cannot start with a group without a clear purpose. You cannot even start endeavours with yourself without a clearly defined purpose. Purpose is everything to everyone and especially to a leader. There's the very popular saying that where the purpose of a thing is unknown, abuse is inevitable. It is so true. The purpose is the driving force of every group. It is the central point. It is the core essence of any group. I have one time talked about knowing the "why" of a thing. The purpose is the "why". I listened to Simon Sinek one time and I loved his exposé on the reason why organisations fail or succeed. He used Apple as a case study. When Apple markets their products, they first tell you the why of their company before telling you what exactly they're into. Today Apple is the most successful computer company simply because they sell from the purpose point.

When people see why you are in business, it makes it easier for them to relate with your product. There is an unconscious trust people attach to you and your product anytime you present your purpose first. It is disastrous to start out an endeavour without clearly defining the purpose of that endeavour. I see this disaster in many people and organisations; why did you decide to invest in that supermarket? Why did you decide to do that genre of music? Why have you started that company? Why are you starting that church?

It is very easy to spot a disaster in the waiting of any person or organization. It doesn't matter if there is a seeming outward appearance of success, purpose is what sustains success. There will always be a tipping point in your life and in the life of that group; the point where you cannot go further without a reference to your purpose. Many people and businesses find themselves in a fight for survival rather than in a thrive to maintain dominance. Yes, there will always be testing moments with life, but those who come out tops from testing times are those who know their purpose, they are those who have had their vision imprinted undeniably in their hearts.

You may argue to say well, there are lots of factors that are responsible for people not being able to reach success and maintain it; resources, marketing strategies, technological advancement and so forth. But I will still show you that all those factors are easily taken care of when there is a clear pursuit of vision and an undeniable sense of purpose. I had to research top companies in the US that were once the stories to tell but have fizzled out of the competition. These companies were once household names for the products they sold, but in especially the past decade, they had plunged downwards in loss and have dwindled or are presently dwindling away because they cannot survive the market.

I grew up knowing Sonny as the number one name in electronics. One time, every electronic device in my home was Sonny. Dad had everything of Sonny. Not more than a decade ago, the Walkman was in fact the only music player device affordable for nearly everyone. Sonny made the transition from VHS to VCD and probably DVD, but with the surge of technological advancements that have drastically overshadowed the popularity of CD's and CD players, Sonny failed to make the much needed transition that would have cemented its place as the number one name in electronics. Needless to say, LG, SAMSUNG and APPLE have blown past Sonny. What went wrong? You could point out many reasons such as failure to transit technological staff, heavy investment in hardware and all that. But it all boils down to purpose.

You see, one thing purpose those is that it keeps you thinking on how to be ahead at what you have started out to do. One time I heard it was said about a top executive at LG that he remarked "We want to be the only name in household appliances". There you go. Have you wondered why you feel comfortable buying a refrigerator from LG and still go on to buy their Smart TV for hundreds of thousands? You might ask what relationship does a TV and a refrigerator have? How can one company make those two different things and still succeed at them both? It all comes down to the purpose of the company. They have said they want to be the only name in household appliances and that's what they're out doing. They know that there are lots of other names that produce household appliances, but to be the number one name LG has to be ahead of the competition.

Purpose is everything. It determines what steps you take in your career and your life. It determines who you hire, who you fire, what you invest in, who you deal with and how you deal with people. Purpose shows the real reason behind every endeavour. I must say at this point that making money or profit alone is never an excellent purpose. The chase for money will certainly derail any group and influence wrong choices, but the chase for a better purpose like adding some kind of value to people, will always end up attracting money.

SUMMARY AND ACTION POINTS

- Define your purpose before you start out. You must know why exactly your group or business exists

- To have an excellent group, your purpose must be something beyond what everyone else strives for. Go for something different. Go for a higher calling

- Making profit and money alone is never a good purpose. Think of something more valuable. Think of people. What value will your group add to people?

II.   PLAN

The other thing is planning. I am yet to see an excellent organization that has succeeded without a plan.

Well, you can say that everyone plans. Before a group starts out, they know exactly what they want so they plan with what they have and plan on how to achieve. But it is one thing to have a plan, and then it is another to have a good plan. What is a good plan? When you set out to do something and you plan to the extent that you know what you have and what you will achieve with your present capacity and abilities, then fair enough to say you have a plan. But when you take the step further to consider what you do not have, how you will organize at a place you have not reached, what you will do if all your initial efforts fall through, then we can start saying you have a good plan. A good plan covers the future; it makes projections and anticipates drastic changes.

A good plan will make provisions for a worst case scenario while believing in a better tomorrow. Many people and groups stop at having a plan and always stick with the cliché that tomorrow will handle its own issues. That's a poor thinking that will never see anyone rise above average. When you start a business for instance, and you have made all the perfect plans on how to make profit in the short-term, and your plan has probably covered to the point where your business would have been well established and self-sustaining. The question would always arise: so what next? After making your turnover and the business is working steadily, what next? This is where the good plan comes in. I must say that the question what next is never for those who never want to be on top. It is not for those who have small dreams. The question is not for those who feel contented with doing what everybody does. The question what next? Is for those who dream and think excellence. I am pretty sure that if DANGOTE had stopped at where everyone else stopped with cement production he would never had become one of the world's richest men.

It all comes down to purpose and that's why I have plan and purpose together under one heading. The purpose you have will influence the kind of plan you make. If your purpose is average, you will only make average plans. Everyone enters into business to make money and that's why most people and organisations are on the same level. But those organisations and people who look beyond money to forge a more valuable purpose will draw up plans that everyone else never draws up and that would take them to heights inexplicable to the normal people.

SUMMARY AND ACTION POINTS

- The kind of purpose you have will influence the kind of plan you make. Your plan is tied to your purpose.

- To be excellent, make good plans that are different from the plans everyone else makes. Your plans should cover areas of the future that others' plans have not considered.

III.　PEOPLE

A team is a group of people who work together to reach the same goal because they share the same vision.

I love football and I am a big fan of Chelsea FC of England and the Super Eagles of Nigeria. Football for me is a near perfect example of what a team is and how to gather the best people. Before I use football to explain how important the best team is to making an excellent group, let me first state a few things;

The best team is not necessarily made of the best people

Quality is more important than quantity in making the best team

A great team is only average without a great leader

***The best team is not necessarily made up of the best people**

It is normal to see businesses and corporations hire the best qualified professionals. No one prefers a mediocre. No one wants to work with people who don't know what they're supposed to do. Everyone appreciates when people work with competence and satisfy the reasons for their employment. Having the best hands run your show sometimes feels like getting the job done already. Sometime ago, I watched the news and saw a report on Dangote (and why isn't his name in the dictionary already?) building what would become the largest private refinery. And then a lot of the staff he already employed were being sent overseas to be trained in anticipation of the completion of the project. The company needed the best trained people and they got them hired and now they need to increase their training to improve their quality, so they shipped them overseas, and of course to the best available institution for training. It would be very difficult for the company to fail in getting the optimum results when business starts.

In fact, our systems in this world are obsessed with getting the best people. To get a scholarship from the government, you must be the best in academics. To get the best job, you must have graduated top of your class. To be ahead in society, you credentials must carry the best content. You know, it's impossible but I wish everyone could just be the best at everything so everyone could get the best of everything. It is great to be the best and everyone should strive to be the best.

But my deepest concern with this obsession and insistence on getting only the best people to work for you and with you is that there seems to be a huge preference for superficial quality than for innate potential. That is, people tend to be more carried away by what they see without having to consider at all what could be seen.

When it comes to building the best team to raise an excellent group, to pursue purpose, I do not believe that much insistence should be placed on the people with the most obvious best quality. Pursuing purpose is like pursuing life. For any person who has looked beyond financial profit to chase a higher calling of imparting his or her generation and society, it is very dangerous to surrender your vision into the hands of people who have been selected solely on the basis of their qualifications. Many times, the best qualifications do not evidence the best intentions, and in pursuing vision, the best intentions should take priority.

To get the best out of people, they do not necessarily have to be the best people available; the most important ingredient in them should be the desire to pursue your vision with you. My advice to people who hire staff is this: when you interview a candidate for a job, give them an opportunity to ask at least two questions, if one of those questions they get to ask isn't "what is the vision of this company?" or something like that, then don't hire them. If they say they have no questions and are satisfied with all your offers, then don't hire them.

This might be a little bit harsh, but vision is more important than money because vision will produce and sustain money. It cuts across everyone. I work with a lot of charity and non-profit volunteer groups, and I can say that the number one problem with reaching goals in these kinds of groups is getting people to work for charity. I'm a professional attorney, leadership consultant and personal development trainer, I do not joke with my expertise and I ensure to charge the appropriate fees. But every time I meet a client, my first option is to consider how I can be of assistance to that person and see that person's life become better by reason of our meeting. Of course I soon move on to the professional fees part, but not so quickly so as to seem desperate for money and not too slowly so as not to be seen as a "Father Christmas". The point is this: do not dare share your vision with anyone whose most pressing question is "So what's in it for me?" Some people might seem the best qualified people, they may have the best track-records and antecedents, but they may not be the best for your vision. They may be the best people, but they definitely may never make the best team. The best people for your team are those who first seek to pursue your vision before their benefits.

Quality is more important than quantity in making the best team

One of the greatest moments of my life was watching Chelsea FC beat FC Barcelona in the Semi-Final of the UEFA Champions League in 2012. Until that day, I had never watched a game of football under the kind of tension I did that game. I could swear that had Chelsea FC lost that game, I would have had a heart attack. Some matches are like that, the atmosphere around the game mixed with the unveiling twists and turns in events tend to keep spectators in the stadium on their feet and those watching live screens wide-eyed and glued while hanging on the edge of their seats. That was how it was. But what's important to us now with respect to that game aren't all the feelings it gave me and millions of other football fans around the world, but the lessons of excellent teamwork I took away from the match. That game, like many other pulsating football matches before it and after it, showed and proved that in success with teams, the quality of your team is more important than the number of players you display.

Here's how Graham Hunter of the UEFA official website reported the match later that evening of April 24th. Let's look at it for our reading pleasure and the takeaway of lessons:

"FC Barcelona 2-2 Chelsea FC (agg: 2-3)

Trailing 2-0 and down to ten men, the visitors hit back with a remarkable rearguard action to reach the final, Fernando Torres sealing it in added time.

Ten-man Chelsea FC pulled off a remarkable rearguard action to reach the 2012 UEFA Champions League final.

Trailing 2-0 to FC Barcelona, they were heading through after Ramires pulled one back with a delicious chip before Fernando Torres made sure on the break in added time.

The writing looked on the wall for the visitors when, having had their 1-0 first-leg lead wiped out by Sergio Busquets, captain John Terry was sent off on 37 minutes. Andrés Iniesta promptly put Barcelona in front on aggregate, only for Ramires to return Chelsea to the box seat before half-time and, despite Lionel Messi hitting the woodwork twice, once from a penalty, in the second period they held on until Torres confirmed progress.

By the time the breakthrough goal came in this extraordinary game Petr Čech had already pulled off a fine one on one save from Messi, both Gerard Piqué and Gary Cahill had departed with injuries and the crowd had roared their throats hoarse. Isaac Cuenca forced the first goal, taking a pass from substitute Daniel Alves and cutting the ball across perfectly for Busquets to steer it past Čech.

The keeper was causing his own attacking problems with his long clearances to lone frontman Didier Drogba, but Terry's departure after an off-the-ball incident involving Alexis Sánchez provided more immediate concern. The tide of pressure and opportunities, already ferocious, looked set to overwhelm Roberto Di Matteo's team. No matter how hard Chelsea worked, there seemed to be two or three Barcelona players around them harassing and then combining with crisp passing movements.

From that came the second goal. Busquets turned the ball over in midfield and freed Sánchez, who rolled it into the path of Messi on the run. The forward has 63 goals to his name this season but when he saw Iniesta better placed he had only one thing in mind, teeing up his team-mate to calmly curve the ball into the Chelsea net.

It takes special stuff to be trailing 2-0, down to ten men and still conjure a response – so hats off to Chelsea. As he had done just before half-time in London last week Frank Lampard ventured forward, found space and clipped a perfect pass to Ramires. The Brazilian displayed sangfroid of which Pelé or Romário would have been proud, deftly lobbing over the advancing Víctor Valdés.

Any expectation that the wind might be taken from Barcelona's sails was dispelled almost immediately after the restart. Drogba's trip on Cesc Fàbregas brought a penalty but while Čech feinted to go this way and that, Messi smashed his effort against the crossbar. Chelsea's attempts to repel any further danger were heroic, trying to compensate for Terry's absence.

Messi was not prepared to depart the competition meekly and late in the game he cracked in a firm shot that Čech touched against the base of his post – it just was not to be.

To cap it all, substitute Torres sprinted clear as Barcelona sought the winner, rounding Valdés and finding the net. Chelsea are on their way to Munich, though there they will be without suspended quartet Ramires, Raul Meireles, Branislav Ivanović and Terry."

The whole essence of this replay is to point out that in succeeding with teams; the quality of the group is more beneficial than the number of group members. Fc Barcelona had the best team in the world with the world's best player Lionel Messi leading their attack, they had a complete team of eleven players while Chelsea Fc were one man short and with no natural central defender on the field. Yet on that epic night, quality triumphed over quantity.

The will to win, the desire succeed, the belief in the big picture inspired an extraordinary display of near perfect teamwork for Chelsea Fc and the club wrote its name in the European history books of football. The resolute stance of the team proved to be the perfect quality that outplayed the best players in the world out-smarted the most decorated coach in football history. When a team buys into the vision and purpose of a course, only that team can stop itself from reaching its set goals and targets.

What is quality?

Do not confuse credentials and robust experience for the essential definition of quality. Of course the qualifications of a person serve as the point of reference for approval when looking out for their suitability in recruitment. But with teamwork, with assembling a group that has to succeed only as a group, the personal credentials of individual members matter for little. What determines the quality of the people is their ability to buy into the course. It is their dedication to the collective vision and resolution to surrender personal goals for collective goals that shows their true quality. This quality is the relevant factor in determining the success of the team.

So, for leaders for hope to inspire their people to achieving success with them, the questions you must ask yourself: What are my criteria for choosing my team? Have I been able to sell the vision to my people? Do I have people who are willing to buy into the vision?

And for those of us who already work with or intend to work with some team for some course, the questions before us: What is the vision? What does the vision mean to me? Am I willing to surrender my personal goals for the vision?

What is quality?

****A great team is only average without a great leader***

An Army of Dogs led by a Lion will Fight like Lions and an Army of Lions led by a Dog will Die Like Dogs - - Imran Khan

Funny but so true it is; you take an average leader and give him or her excellent followers, the whole team will end up as average. But you take a leader who's got the right passion, vision and a clear purpose and put him or her in charge of average followers, you will no doubt end up having a great team. A great leader will transfer greatness to his people. It's the law of influence at work. You can only emit what you contain.

Here again, football would serve as a good example for explanations. If you have all the best players in the world in one team and give them an average coach, that team will end up as an average team except some great player in the team rises up to the occasion and takes the leadership role of spreading the right influence. Leadership is influence and influence all the way.

Leaders must always improve on their capacities and show themselves competent in vision and purpose and in ability to transfer their passions to their people. Leaders must always be ready to show their people how dedicated and passionate they are, and when this is done with consistency, the attitude is transferred and the right people are attracted.

No matter how good you are as a follower, no matter the great potentials you may have, no matter the excellent qualities at your disposal, if you follow an average leader, average is the destination. You can never fly to the moon in a helicopter, you need a space ship. That's how teamwork and leadership works, you will never reach success as a team when your leader is not made or prepared for success. This is why as followers; we must always ensure we have the growth plan that helps us develop our capacity because there is no void in life. Whenever there is a need for leadership at any level, only those prepared for it will get the beckon to takeover. Every follower is a leader, first of himself and then of his team. So whatever it takes, don't settle for average as a leader and never let average be your standard as a follower.

SUMMARY AND ACTION POINTS

- Are you a people oriented leader and follower? You must constantly remind yourself that people are the most important aspects of your destiny. You can never achieve greatness as a team without the right people around you.

- What is the quality of your people? A great team on paper is never always the great team in the game. You must define quality by the amount of dedication to the purpose of the team. If people work for your team just because they have some personal gain to realise, then chances are that no matter how good they may be in their qualifications, they may never be very useful to the team in moments that demand teamwork.

- Are you average or are you great? All leaders and followers must constantly try to keep growing their capacities. You cannot lead the future while living in the past. You must grow to remain relevant.

IV.   PICTURE

"…If a blind man leads a blind man, both will fall into a pit." Matthew 15:14b

What could be worse than a leader having followers but being without vision? I think only a few terrible things in life could.

In the first place, to be able to garner the followership of people, you must have a clear picture of where you're headed. It's easier for people to follow you when they have an idea of where you're headed, but it's extremely easier for people to follow you when they have a clear picture of where you're headed.

Two sets of Eyes

Human beings are visual creatures, we respond faster to things we see than to other things. And that's why most of our information and communication gadgets come with screens. We act more when we see than when we feel. In fact, many times, what we see trigger how we feel.

As humans, we are created with two sets of eyes – our naked eyes and our clothed eyes. Of course the naked eyes are the eyes we use in seeing physical stuff and experiencing our environment. But our clothed eyes are what we could otherwise refer to as our mind's eyes. Our naked eyes help us feel human. We perceive our physical environment with our eyes and gain direction. Movement if easier when the naked eyes are working. Speed is added to motion when the eyes are directly involved in movement. It is difficult to make progress when the eyes are shut. One of the most terrible disabilities a person could ever suffer is blindness. I remember one time, a couple I used to know had a baby and a few days after the birth of the child, the baby fell sick. Fever was high and the baby was always crying. After some examination with the doctors, it was discovered that the baby was blind. Such a terrible situation. That's how important the eyes are. Your whole body could come down with sickness just because your eyes are blind.

When you think of the disadvantage blindness brings, you begin to wonder how people who are blind cope. But you know there are lots of blind people who have been able to cope pretty well with their situation. Many of them even live much better lives than people who have no blindness. We have blind musicians and artistes who have impacted the entertainment industry with great skill and have made a good name and a good living for themselves even with their being blind. This makes a point clear: real blindness is the blindness of the mind. It is terrible to be blind in the naked eyes, but it is inevitably disastrous to be blind in the mind's eye. People can be blind but still can have a great sense of vision and purpose. It is this great sense of vision that distinguishes an excellent team from an average team.

Every group of people pursuing an endeavour must have a clear picture of what they pursue. A team cannot head into any endeavour without knowing exactly the goal of their entrance.

SUMMARY AND ACTION POINTS

- What's the picture before you? Have clarity of purpose first to be able to clearly show others the purpose.

- Do your people also have clarity with the direction you're headed? Paint the picture of the vision to everyone on the team and get them to understand clearly where the team is going.

V.   PURSUIT

A wise man once said "great messages don't change people, great decisions do". I couldn't agree less. What's the benefit of a great vision without action?

When I talk about vision to leaders, I usually love to quote from Habakkuk 2:2. It's one of my favourite Bible verses and it pretty much tells the "vision story" in a simple self-explanatory way. I'll quote that verse here again…

"Write the vision, make it plain upon tablets, that he may run that readeth it" Habakkuk 2:2 (King James Version).

Talking about taking action with your team, the relevant part of that verse says "…he may run that readeth it"

You cannot see results with your team if you do not run with your dream. A vision is as good as how much pursuit you put into it. The world does not reward good intentions. The world rewards good results.

Ever wondered why in football coaches are sacked very often? Well, the thing is, sports teams are result oriented every team has got a vision for their year. Teams start out with ambitions for each business year, and they hire coaches to lead their teams to reaching their ambitions. So from the onset the vision is laid out for the coach and he is tasked with the responsibility of using the available resources in the team to achieve the goals laid out for him. If at the end of the year the goals are not reached, his work will be reviewed, and if it appears that he's failed, then he would be fired. That's how it works. The actions of pursuing the goals are so important that even before the end of the business year, if results look like the goals may not be achieved or the coach seems likely to fail, he would be fired.

That's how important actions are to goals and visions. The question then is, "how can leaders effectively pursue the team visions to at least get a chance of success?"

*Take Responsibility for the Vision

It starts with the leader. You must assume full responsibility for reaching the goals. You must first take ownership of the vision before trying to get others buy into it. Your daily actions must show a real commitment to making the goal work. Your people must not have a hard time trying to find where to get inspiration from to pursue the goal. You are the one to initiate every plan, agenda and action. You've got to first take responsibility. It is irresponsible to demand responsibility from others without first taking responsibility.

*Show Commitment to the Vision

The leader it is who is the first to get involved. A team is only as committed as its leader. Many leaders especially volunteer organisations always complain of the lack of commitment of the people they try to recruit. There is always the feeling passed on that nobody really wants to put in their best in doing the work. Most times, you look at the leaders who complain, you observe from them a lack of show of real commitment. The best way to build a committed team is to be an example of true commitment. People learn from examples they see. You cannot get people to buy into something you do not believe in.

How do you show commitment? Be the first in all things! When you fix a meeting, be the first to show up. When you fix a deadline, be the first to meet it. When you ask for volunteers, be the first to volunteer. When you ask for donations, be the first to make a donation. And always make it known to the team that you are the first. When you show commitment this way, it becomes clear to the team that their leader is in true pursuit of the vision. It becomes easier for them the join in the pursuit of the vision.

*Share the Responsibility with everyone in the team

After showing responsibility and commitment, you have now earned the right to ask others to take responsibility too. Everyone in the team must have a role to play in pursuing the vision. You cannot afford to leave anyone in the loop. Everyone must have something they should be held responsible for. When responsibility is shared, there is a buy-in to the vision. People in the team can begin to breed a sense of ownership of the vision. It is easier to reach the goal when everyone feels part of the process and feels responsible one way or another for the achievement of the goals.

Demand Commitment from everyone

I remember one time former Chelsea Coach Jose Mourinho was talking about his untouchable starting eleven and he talked about former Chelsea midfield maestro Michael Essien. The Coach said of Essien that every time he steps on the pitch, he gave "a hundred and ten percent".

That's what it means to be committed – giving more than what is required. People who give only what is required are simply involved in the team. But those who go the extra mile are those who are committed. To get the best out of your team, you must demand the extra from everyone. You must demand commitment.

SUMMARY AND ACTION POINTS

- What are you doing everyday about your vision? What is your team doing to see you vision succeed? A great vision without great actions is failure in disguise.

- As the leader, are you taking responsibility for the vision? Are you being an example of commitment? Does everyone in the team feel a sense of ownership of the vision? How many people in your team can you say give 110% every time you demand commitment?

A Final Word

I am now not saying that if all the above principles are applied straight-jacket then success is inevitable. No! These days, you could all the right things and a pandemic shows up one morning and all your work is back to ground zero. But what I am saying is, to give your team a great chance at success, the essentials shared in this book must be taken seriously.

I think that teamwork might just be the most difficult aspect of leadership, maybe next to self-leadership. Dealing with yourself alone as a leader is tough. Many leaders still find it pretty hard to navigate through their personal development effectively. The process of self-discipline is still something of a mountain for most leaders. And so it becomes a herculean task for leaders to transfer what they are not. A leader who finds it difficult to craft his own purpose cannot help his team craft their purpose. A leader with poor values by himself cannot become a people person to attract the right set of people. A leader who lacks clarity of vision cannot cast a vision for his team, he will find it hard to run with any other vision.

This boils out on every member of the team. I believe that everyone is a leader, and every team is a collection of leaders differentiated by their levels of influence. So, the team must have great individual leaders who are effective in the five essentials treated in this book to be able to form an excellent group. Organisations are drawn back by the failures of individuals, and that's why many organisations expend much resources in training their people to improve on a personal level, because they know that failure on the personal level will translate to failure on the team level.

A team is as strong as its weakest member. No matter how cool and great individual members of the team may look at their individual levels, if they cannot translate their individual greatness into the collective, they will never make up a great team. So, the key is in the individual. Get it right with the people individually, and you get it right with the team collectively.

Notes

Other books by the author...
VISION
THE CORE
HOW TO BEAT YOUR LEADER
To place an order for e-copies or hardcopies of these works...
Call today! - +2347086668850
Or reach Precious on Facebook @iPreciousEda
Or visit preciouseda.blogspot.com
Precious Eda
#1 Millennial in Leadership

Precious
Eda
#iLEADERSHIP

www.ingramcontent.com/pod-product-compliance
Lightning Source LLC
LaVergne TN
LVHW050427160726
843469LV00041B/1256